For my niece, Lizzy. *H.W.*

First published in Great Britain 2023 by Red Shed,
part of Farshore

An imprint of HarperCollins*Publishers*
1 London Bridge Street
London SE1 9GF
www.farshore.co.uk

HarperCollins*Publishers*
Macken House, 39/40 Mayor Street Upper, Dublin 1
D01 C9W8

Text and illustrations copyright © HarperCollins*Publishers* 2023
ISBN 978 0 0085 2441 8
Printed in the UK by Bell and Bain Ltd, Glasgow.
001

Consultancy by Dr Miquela Walsh, DEdPsych, MsC (Dist),
BSc (Hons), HCPC accredited.

A CIP catalogue record for this book is available from the British Library.

Stay safe online. Any website addresses listed in this book are correct at the time
of going to print. However, Farshore is not responsible for content hosted by third
parties. Please be aware that online content can be subject to change and websites
can contain content that is unsuitable for children. We advise that all children are
supervised when using the internet.

MIX
Paper | Supporting
responsible forestry
FSC™ C007454

This book is produced from independently certified FSC™ paper
to ensure responsible forest management.

For more information visit: www.harpercollins.co.uk/green

Hannah Wilson

Samara Hardy

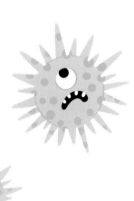

WORRIES BiG AND SMALL WHEN YOU ARE 8

RED SHED

What if . . .

What if I worry about stuff?

A worry is an uncomfortable feeling about a situation. Perhaps a feeling of fear about speaking in front of the class or of nervousness about seeing the dentist. EVERYBODY worries about stuff. Big stuff, little stuff, all kinds of stuff. You might think some of your worries are silly. They're NOT. All worries are important as they can stop us from doing things.

Worries are a normal part of life. We can't get rid of all of them, but we can stop them bossing us around. The best way to deal with a worry is to TALK ABOUT IT with a grown-up you trust. In this book, I call this person 'your grown-up'. Your grown-up is probably your mum, dad or the person who looks after you – or all three! You can tell your grown-up (or grown-ups) ANYTHING. It can be hard talking about things that worry us, but it's lovely to get a hug and a thank you for being so brave for sharing our feelings. So let's get chatting about tricky stuff and stop worries getting in the way of fun!

WORRIES BOTHER US AT DIFFERENT AGES.
IF YOU ARE OLDER OR YOUNGER THAN EIGHT,
THIS BOOK IS STILL FOR YOU!

What if the dentist check-up hurts?

A check-up is a QUICK LOOK at your teeth. It won't hurt. But it may feel a little odd opening your mouth like a YAWNING HIPPO while gloved fingers poke around!

If you need a treatment, perhaps a filling or a deep clean, talk about any worries with your grown-up. The dentist will expertly work to keep your teeth healthy and keep YOU comfortable. It's great news that your gnashers are being looked after, so hop on that chair and make like a HIPPO!

What if my friend gives me sweets, but I'm not allowed them?

Perhaps you REALLY wanted to eat them, but didn't? Or did you gobble them up and then feel bad? Whatever the situation, whatever the worry, talk about it with your grown-up, even if you think you did something wrong. They will be impressed by your HONESTY (telling the truth).

Sometimes it's hard to know what to do, especially if your grown-up isn't there. They don't expect you to be perfect, just like THEY aren't perfect. So they probably won't be cross. They'll be proud of you for sharing the worry so you can chat about how to make good decisions.

What if the car or bus is noisy and bumpy?

It's normal for cars, buses, trains and aeroplanes to WOBBLE and BOUNCE, creak, squeak, rumble and bang. These movements and sounds happen when engines start, or the vehicles drive over bumps, or fly through rough patches in the air called TURBULENCE. All vehicles are checked by mechanics to make sure they're safe. So sit back and ENJOY THE RIDE!

What if my grown-up breaks a rule?

When I was little, I used to go the park with my dad. There were DO NOT WALK ON THE GRASS signs. So what did my dad do? You guessed it! I worried he would get in BIG trouble. But my dad understood the CONSEQUENCES (what happens next) of his action. (He had to say sorry to the park warden!)

Ask your grown-up if THEY understand the consequences of their actions. If they say YES, then throw your worries in the park bin. Let them handle their actions, while you handle yours.

What if I feel angry?

We all do from time to time. Anger is a normal EMOTION (feeling). But is being angry HELPFUL? Think about a time when you got angry. What did the anger make you say or do? Were those things helpful? If we shout horrible things or hit people, the anger is HARMFUL to ourselves and others. How can we stop this?

CONTROL ANGER: We can't get rid of it completely, but we can learn to manage it. How can you calm down next time you feel angry? I walk away from the situation and take deep breaths. Later, I think about what happened and I might chat to someone.

UNDERSTAND ANGER: Think about how your body feels when you start to get angry, so you can recognize it more quickly next time. And think about WHY you get angry. Sometimes, when we are upset on the inside, we get angry on the outside.

TOP TIPS TO CALM DOWN:

1. Walk away
2. Take deep breaths
3. Slowly count to 10

Are you upset about anything? Telling your grown-up about worries is a good way to release them, so they don't bubble up inside you and burst out as anger. Like lemonade exploding from a bottle! Teaching anger who's the boss (that's YOU) needs practice, so keep trying. Good luck!

What if I feel so sad that I don't want to do anything?

Sadness is also normal. We ALL feel it and we can't get rid of all sad feelings. It doesn't feel nice, but sadness shows that we are thoughtful, caring people. If our friend moves away, we might feel sad because we care about that person and we'll miss them. But if we are so sad we don't feel like doing anything, we must try to deal with it. But HOW?

Like anger, sadness can bottle up inside us, but it's not quite as fizzy and explosive as lemonade. What does sadness feel like for YOU?

NOTICING feelings is a good first step towards UNDERSTANDING them.

Sadness can be slow, heavy and tiring, like a bottle of sludgy syrup. Take off the lid and pour some out by TALKING. It's OK to cry too. Tears can also help to release a little sadness.

Then, with your grown-up, think of something fun or relaxing to do. What made you feel better last time you were sad? A puzzle or a trip to the shops? Even if you don't feel like it, GIVE IT A GO.

Often, sadness fades all by itself. That doesn't mean we've stopped caring, it just means we are able to get on with things.

What if my friend says my puppy stickers are babyish?

When we like stuff that younger kids like, it doesn't mean that stuff is babyish. It means it is for EVERYONE. Everyone can have fun with stickers. When your friend called your stickers babyish, that was just their OPINION (something they think). It wasn't a FACT, like two plus two equals four is a fact.

We all have different opinions. Some people love cheese, others think it smells like mouldy socks. If YOU like your puppy stickers, then keep sticking! What could you tell your friend if they say it again? Let them know you can make up your OWN mind!

What if germs make me sick?

All of us get sick from time to time. But medicines can make us better and stop us getting ill. We are unlikely to get VERY ill.

GERMS are teeny-weeny, too small to see, living blobs. Many of them keep us HEALTHY, helping to suck goodness from food or protecting us from illness. Some germs can make us sick while our body battles them. But your BRILLIANT BODY learns how to defend itself, so when some germs pop up again, you won't get sick!

What if someone in my class tells a lie about me?

Were they being mean or did they make a mistake? Maybe they think you really DO live in a submarine (or whatever the not-true thing was). How do you feel about what was said? Embarrassed? Annoyed? If you feel hurt, chat with your grown-up to work out why, and think of ACTIONS that could help.

Can you tell your classmates your side of the story? Your grown-up or teacher could help. Can you hang out with different classmates? Or do you just want to FORGET about it? After a while, EVERYONE will forget. Meanwhile, keep busy with fun activities. What can you tell yourself when life seems unfair and you've just got to get on with it? I like to say, "Bye, bye, worry pie!" (I don't know what it means either!)

You can't control what others say or do, so focus on being AMAZING YOU!

13

What if I think I'm ugly?

We all look different. We can be tall or short, with curly or straight hair, pale or dark skin. We can have large ears and freckles, or small noses and wonky grins. There is no right or wrong way to look on the outside, and everyone has a DIFFERENT OPINION about what is ugly or beautiful.

Think about the dogs in your local park. You might find the small stumpy pooch with the squashed nose beautiful, but your grown-up disagrees. They think the shaggy hound with floppy ears is beautiful. So OUTSIDE beauty and ugliness are a matter of opinion, not fact.

Imagine that the stumpy pooch is always yapping and snapping and chasing squirrels. A bad-tempered doggy! Would you STILL think it was beautiful? It works like this for people too. How someone is on the INSIDE affects how they appear on the outside. When someone is caring, fun and thoughtful, their INNER BEAUTY shines through to the outside.

Real beauty comes from the INSIDE.

As long as you are not a yappy snappy squirrel-chaser, you are NOT ugly. Many people think you're as beautiful as rainbows and snowflakes. So KEEP SMILING and keep letting your inner beauty shine through.

LINE UP SOME TOYS
and practise speaking
out loud to them.

What if I have to speak in front of the class?

This sort of thing gives many of us the wibble-wobbles.
What is making YOU feel wobbly? Looking silly or making
a mistake in front of lots of people? Your classmates
probably feel the same way. They're too busy worrying
about their OWN speech — or daydreaming about
armadillos — to notice YOUR mistakes. Even if they do,
they'll think how BRAVE you are for KEEPING GOING.

So get up there and give it go. The more you do stuff like
this, the easier it will get. It'll be over in a flash, and
you'll be PROUD of your spectacular speaking effort!

What if there's a test tomorrow?

What is worrying you? What might help you feel better? Learning your spellings or science stuff? I know you'd rather be rolling about in the living room, but we're trying to stop worries rolling about inside your HEAD! Being prepared might help.

On the test day, take a DEEP BREATH. Concentrate and GO FOR IT! Then, whatever the result, you can feel proud because you DID YOUR BEST. Great job.

ASK FOR HELP.
We all need a hand
with hard stuff.

What if my friend always does better than me at school?

Sometimes it feels like other people are always better than us. But we are all good at DIFFERENT THINGS. Your friend might be great at painting, but you might be great at reading and sport. What ARE you good at?

It's normal to compare ourselves to others, but it's not helpful if it makes us feel we're not good enough. You ARE good enough. If you want to be even better, compare yourself to YOURSELF. Work on school stuff that's tricky for you. You'll soon feel like a school superstar.

17

What if I'm going to visit someone in hospital?

Before you go, have a good old chat with your grown-up about what might happen during the visit. Ask questions. What would you like to know about? WHY your friend or family member is in hospital? Or what treatment they are having?

You may want to ask how they might LOOK. It's normal to feel a little upset when we see someone we care about looking unwell or different. And if you already know about the machine they are attached to, you won't be too surprised when you see it. Those machines – as well as the kind, clever doctors and nurses – are helping them.

What will you DO at the hospital, do you think? Your loved one might be too poorly for a dance-off, but might love to play cards or have a little chat.

Can you go to the hospital cafe? Let's hope it serves hot chocolate with sprinkles AND marshmallows!

Do you feel more ready for the trip now? Your friend or family member will be SO happy you came to visit. You put aside your own worries to help someone else. What a CARING person you are!

What if another person sees my privates?

'Privates' means the parts of your body under your underwear. They are private, which means they are just for YOU to see and touch. You are in charge of them. Your body belongs to you. If another child accidentally sees your privates (or you see theirs), for example in the changing room at the swimming pool, this is OK. If a doctor needs to examine your private parts at the doctor's surgery or in hospital with your grown-up by your side, this is also OK.

But if a grown-up ever asks or tries to see or touch your privates, that is NOT OK. If a grown-up asks you to look at or touch THEIR private parts, that is NOT OK. Say NO.

Tell your grown-up as soon as you can, even if someone says it's a secret and you mustn't tell. You CAN tell. You can ALWAYS tell your grown-up anything. Anything that makes you feel uncomfortable, anything bad, embarrassing or weird. Even if you think you did something wrong. You haven't done anything wrong and you will NOT get into trouble. Your grown-up will make things better and they'll be so proud of you for telling.

What if my friend is right and my hair does look silly?

I don't think your friend is right. I bet your hair is JUST FINE. They might not really believe what they said. They might just be feeling grumpy. They might even feel SORRY for being mean.

Sometimes people are unkind. We can't control that. But how can we WORRY LESS about what others say? Why not focus on YOU? You can control whether YOU are unkind or not. You can control what YOU say. What could you say if your friend calls your hair silly again? How about: "My hair is FABULOUS!" or "My hair is silly, but I LIKE silly!"

What if a burglar breaks into my house?

This sounds like a bedtime sort of worry. The sort of worry we have when the lights are out and CREEPY NOISES make us imagine all kinds of strange stuff. Am I right? NAUGHTY IMAGINATION!

Let's show it who's boss with some FACTS. Ask your grown-up if your house is safe. I bet it is. I bet it has door locks. Go see for yourself. Then try to find out what is making the funny noises. Is Nibbles the cat wrestling a bush? Is your grown-up a secret tap-dancer? SHH, we're trying to sleep!

What if my grown-ups have an argument?

I'm afraid that arguments are quite common. Just like you, your grown-ups will sometimes shout, cry or say things they don't really mean. How does hearing them argue make you feel? It can be scary to hear adults shouting. So head off to your bedroom, cuddle your teddies and read a book. It's THEIR argument, not yours.

Arguments do NOT mean people don't love each other or that one of them will leave home. Later, when things are calm, can you describe your feelings to your grown-ups? They don't want you to be upset, so they might be able to find ways to stop their arguments worrying you.

Actions that are POSITIVE (good or helpful) can make us feel better.

How about a BAKE SALE to raise money for people affected by war?

What if there's a war?

Most wars don't happen suddenly. They usually build up slowly, over many months or years. So experts know where and when wars might happen. Ask your grown-up if war might take place where YOU live. Most countries are safe and peaceful.

Even if a war DID happen near you, the grown-ups would know beforehand, so you could move to a safe place. Did you hear or see some news about a war? Try to tell your grown-up what worried you about this. You may need a big hug and a reminder that all is well in YOUR world.

What if I die soon?

Sadly, everyone will die one day. That day, for you, is probably a VERY long time from now, when you are very old. It is unusual for children to die. Children's bodies are GREAT at beating illness and injury, helped by doctors and medicines. And your grown-up knows how to keep you safe. Any idea WHY you're thinking about dying? What worries do you have? Remember, you can chat with your grown-up about ANYTHING, even stuff like death.

Calm panic by finding:

3 things you can see
2 things you can hear
1 thing you can touch

Now, put on your apron — we're going to get COOKING! We're going to cook up a cauldron of thoughts about the FUTURE. Nobody really knows what will happen in the future, so we can take charge of how we think about it.

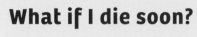

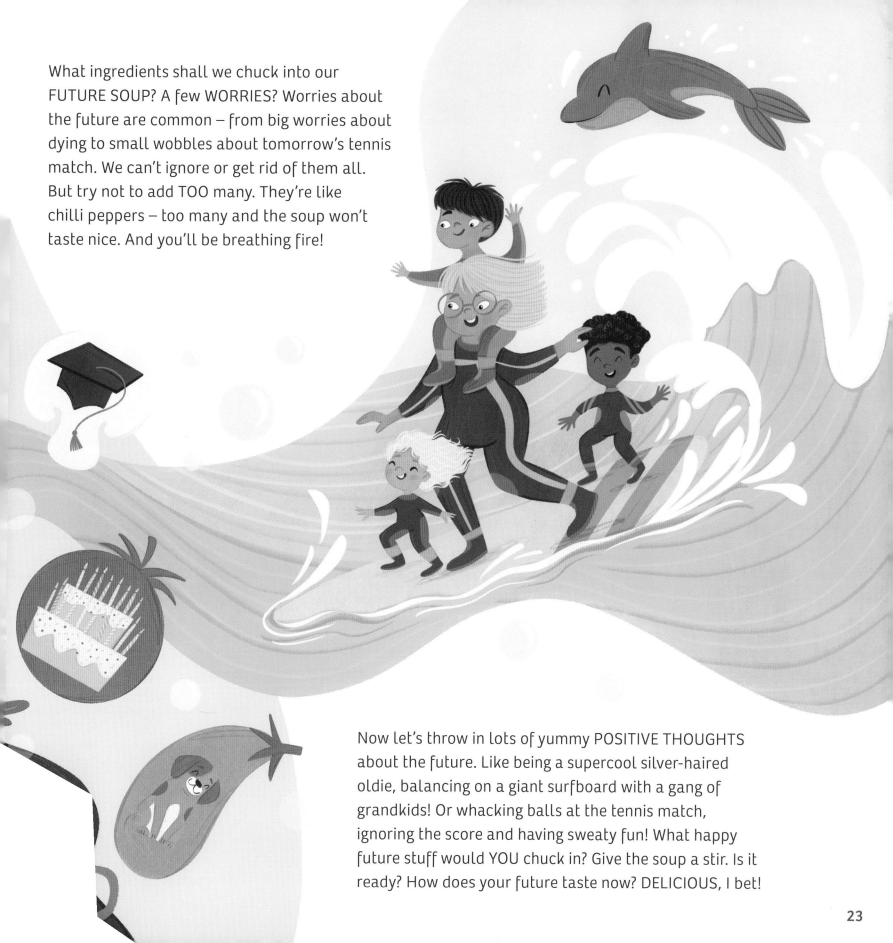

What ingredients shall we chuck into our FUTURE SOUP? A few WORRIES? Worries about the future are common – from big worries about dying to small wobbles about tomorrow's tennis match. We can't ignore or get rid of them all. But try not to add TOO many. They're like chilli peppers – too many and the soup won't taste nice. And you'll be breathing fire!

Now let's throw in lots of yummy POSITIVE THOUGHTS about the future. Like being a supercool silver-haired oldie, balancing on a giant surfboard with a gang of grandkids! Or whacking balls at the tennis match, ignoring the score and having sweaty fun! What happy future stuff would YOU chuck in? Give the soup a stir. Is it ready? How does your future taste now? DELICIOUS, I bet!

23

What if all my friends have their own device, but I don't?

Are you sure ALL your friends have a phone, laptop or tablet? I bet some of them don't. But I do know it can feel tough when others have something we want. That tough feeling is JEALOUSY.

What else have you felt jealous about? Do you think anyone has ever felt jealous of YOU? It's a normal feeling, but quite tricky to deal with. We have to try to accept that different people have different things. Would it help to understand WHY you don't have a device? Ask your grown-up. Remember, they're not being mean – they're doing what they think is best for you.

What if I see something weird on the internet?

When we use the internet, we bring the big wide world into our OWN world. Sometimes stuff meant only for adults pops up. Kids may find these pictures, videos or messages weird, confusing, embarrassing or scary. Has this happened to YOU? Or did you click on something strange or watch something that felt naughty? Or did you share messages with a stranger or give out personal information?

No matter what you saw or did, TELL YOUR GROWN-UP. You won't be in trouble and they won't take away your device. They'll be pleased you told them. Chat about how the experience made you feel and how to surf the internet safely.

If you feel uncomfortable or unsure about anything online, CHECK with your grown-up.

SHARE your online world with your grown-up.

NEVER be mean online. Digital footprints last forever.

What if someone is mean to me online?

Did they post a mean message or an embarrassing photo? Did your friends gang up on you in a game? How did it make you FEEL? Sad, angry or lonely?

When someone is mean for a long time – even online – it's bullying. Bullying is NEVER your fault. We can sometimes ignore a mean word or two, but it's hard to deal with bullying on our own. So tell your grown-up and make a plan. Can you delete messages, block the person or ask someone to talk to them? If your device is taking over or causing worries, show it who's boss – SWITCH IT OFF for a while and find fun IRL (In Real Life)!

What if my pet died and I'm very sad?

I'm really sorry your pet has died. Can you talk to your grown-up about anything that's troubling you, perhaps WHY your pet died or what happened with the vet?

When my hamster Ernie died, my family was too sad to pack away his cage immediately. We wrote goodbye messages inside hearts and left them on the cage for a few days. Would a goodbye ceremony help YOU, even if your pet died a while ago?

Let your feelings go up and down like a rollercoaster. It's OK to feel sad, grumpy, happy, ANYTHING. One day, you'll be able to think about your pet calmly. They are gone, but your love for them is here forever.

Make a scrapbook of memories.

What if some things are just for boys and some things are just for girls?

GOOD NEWS: Everything is for EVERYONE! No matter who you are, you can climb mountains, play football, dance, or be a chef or scientist. It doesn't matter what anyone else thinks. So get tackling and twirling, baking and experimenting! Climb high and GO FOR IT!

What if I get lost in the supermarket?

That's a good question! Have you asked your grown-up? What should YOU do and what should THEY do? Work out answers before you next go. That way, you'll know whether to stay where you are, ask a shop worker for help or meet by the cabbages!

You can also chat about ways not to get lost in the first place. Don't let what-if worries bounce around inside your head — try to let them out by TALKING. When you have answers and action plans, worries won't bounce around quite so much.

What if I don't want to go to school?

School can be tricky sometimes, can't it? What do you find difficult? Your grown-up or teacher can help make some things less tricky for you. Other tricky things — like finding school YAWN-TASTICALLY boring — you just have to get on with. We all need to do things we don't feel like from time to time. School is good for you. If you can work out WHY, you might feel more like going.

Is there any FUN stuff? Perhaps fish-and-chip Fridays or storytime? Pop those POSITIVES in your pocket and give school another chance. Good effort!

What if I've got a sleepover soon?

WOWEE, that should be fun! Let's get you ready.
It's NORMAL to have the wobbles about sleepovers.
Many of us feel nervous about staying away from
home for the night, especially if it's somewhere new.

Being prepared can help, so could
your friend come to a sleepover at YOUR
house first? Practise being sleepover buddies!

Or could you go to their house for a DAYTIME playdate?
Your pal could show you where you would sleep for a sleepover.
What else would you want to know about? Their house and bedtime
routine will seem different – your friend might even wear socks to bed!
But different becomes familiar pretty quickly, so give new things a go.

With your grown-up, ask and answer some what-if questions. For example, "What if I can't get to sleep?" Answer: "I would read a book." Or "What if I don't want a bath?" Answer: "It's OK to stay stinky." Or "What if I need a wee in the middle of the night?" Answer: "I would tickle my friend awake and ask them to take me." What are YOUR what-if plans?

It's fine for a few wobbles to come with you on the sleepover, but you'll probably forget them when you're having fun with your friend – fingers crossed for popcorn and a movie! The sleepover will help you build up your SELF-CONFIDENCE and discover that different is OK. Nice bed socks!